3

a F
b T
c T
d T
e T
f F
g F
h T
i T
j T
k F
l F

9 Opinions

Grammar

1

Student's own answers.

2

a His mother said that life was like a box of chocolates.
b Freddy told the children that he was coming for them.
c He told Fredo that he had broken his heart.
d She said that his eyes had made love to her all evening.
e He said that he would be back.
f He said that he was going to make him an offer that he couldn't refuse.
g She said that she had had a farm in Africa.
h Her told her that they would always have Paris.

3 **My favorite movie is *Titanic*. I've already seen it six times and I'm going to watch it again tonight. I'm a great fan of Kate Winslet and I'm hoping to meet her one day. I particularly like the ending, although it always makes me cry. I don't find Leonardo DiCaprio very attractive, but I think he is a great actor.**

4

a ✓
b She asked me what the title of his last book was.
c ✓
d She asked me which book I had read first.
e She asked me if I was going to read any of his books again.
f ✓
g She asked me if I knew anything about his life.
h ✓

a Who is your favorite living author?
b What was the title of his last book?
c How many books has he written?
d Which book did you read first?
e Will you read any of his books again? / Are you going to read any of his books again?
f Have you read all his books?
g Do you know anything about his life?
h What are you reading now?

5

a She asked me if I had enjoyed it.
b She asked me who the main characters were.
c She asked me how the story began.
d She asked me if I would like to read it again.
e She asked me what I would read next.
f She asked me if anyone had recommended the book to me.
g She asked me if it was easy to get into.
h She asked me if I ever stopped reading a book before the end.

Vocabulary

1

a photography
b ending
c tearjerker
d subtitles
e soundtrack
f set in
g thriller

2

a	b	c	d	e	f	g	h
3	2	1	4	5	8	7	6

3

a
1 all
2 track
3 reggae
4 live
5 gig
6 lyrics
7 speakers

b
1 techno
2 hip-hop
3 classical
4 opera
5 orchestra
6 band
7 dance

4

1 novel
2 gripping
3 put
4 chapters
5 get
6 character
7 plot
8 ending
9 cover
10 paperback

5

a annoying
b bored
c challenging
d confused
e disappointed
f exciting
g fascinating
h relaxed
i inspired

6

1 d
2 a
3 e
4 f
5 c
6 b
7 h
8 g

Pronunciation

1

a die ✓
b file ✓
c late ✓

d mine ✓
e tape ✓
f wait ✓

2

/eɪ/	/aɪ/
age	buy
change	child
claim	cry
date	guy
great	mind
save	night
strange	quite
way	wild

Writing

1

the cast ✓
the plot ✓
the soundtrack ✓

2

a I was especially impressed by
b I thoroughly recommend it.
c The movie tells the story of
d Set in
e It stars
f the plot is not always easy to understand
g that was a big hit

10 Childhood

Grammar

1

a ~~which~~
b ~~who~~
c ~~who~~
d ~~which~~
e ~~which~~
f ~~which~~
g ~~who~~

2

a My dad is a nice guy who gives me lots of presents.
b Dad lives with a new girlfriend who doesn't like me.
c She has a daughter who I sometimes play with.
d They have a house by the ocean that I really like.
e My mom and I have a small apartment that she's really proud of.
f Mom has a job which doesn't pay very well.
g She works for a man who looks like my father.
h This is a picture of my dad that I drew.

3

a unless
b if
c if
d If
e unless
f unless
g unless

4

a You'll never find a good job if you don't go to college.
e You shouldn't have children if you don't have a lot of money.
f Life is very hard if you don't come from a rich family.
g Children never learn if you don't yell at them from time to time.

5

a Do you know why ~~did Hayley run~~ Hayley ran away from home?
b Can you tell me if this was the first time?
c Do you ~~think~~ know if she's been sick recently?
d Could you tell me if ~~does she have~~ she has a boyfriend?
e Do you know where she ~~did go~~ went?
f Do you think that she is having problems at school?
g Do you have any idea ~~will she~~ if she will do it again?

6

a Do you think children have too much freedom?
b Do you have any idea where your son is now?
c Can you tell me if your child is under stress at school?
d Could you tell me what your children think of you?
e Do you know if your children are happy?
f Do you think school is more important than the family in a child's education?

Vocabulary

1

a at
b up
c about
d off
e up
f of
g in
h up

2

a take care of
b brought up
c telling off
d worry about
e sat up
f tuck in
g yell at
h cleaning up

3

a did your parents make you do the dishes?
b did they let you have a cell phone?
c did they let you eat dinner in front of the TV?
d did they make you clean up your room?
e did they let you watch horror movies?
f did they let you sleep at a friend's house?

4

a My parents made me go to church every Sunday.
b The boss never lets us take a day off.
c I don't let the dog come into the house.
d You're going to make me get angry.
e They didn't let us have any freedom.
f Will you let me to come with you?
g Don't make her talk if she doesn't want to.

5

1 for
2 use
3 like
4 looks
5 with
6 of
7 thing

Workbook Answer Key

7 News

Grammar

1

- a being
- b me
- c to have
- d reading
- e spending
- f to get
- g to help
- h to go

2

- a He warned me not to touch it.
- b She promised that she would be there at eight. / She promised to be there at eight.
- c He suggested that I sue the photographers.
- d She explained to me that the interest rate changes from time to time.
- e I realized that I had better not leave this job.
- f He told his wife to forget about him.
- g She agreed to see them both later.
- h He asked her to stop being mean.

3

- a was
- b be
- c Are
- d were
- e Have
- f Is
- g being
- h been

4

- a was arrested
- b was stopped
- c were found
- d has been arrested
- e has never been convicted
- f was kept
- g was canceled / has been
- h is believed

5

- a The car was followed by the paparazzi for ten kilometers.
- b She is photographed by people when she walks down the street.
- c She will be paid $50,000 by the newspaper for the pictures.
- d The pictures will be put on the front page of the newspaper.
- e Last night, an enormous sum of money was stolen by thieves from a Hollywood celebrity.
- f The football player, Ed Flower, has been accused by police officers of burglary.

6

- a Donovan Thomas ~~was~~ escaped from prison in Rhode Island, in the US, after serving 89 days of a 90-day sentence. He was caught and sentenced to an extra six months.
- b Philip Johnson, 32, from Prestonburg, Kentucky, shot himself in the chest because he wanted to see if it hurt. He ~~was~~ discovered that it hurts a lot.
- c Circus girl, Jasmine Brown, 22, was jailed for six days by a court in San Diego. She was riding an elephant on a busy highway and she was not wearing any clothes.
- d André Gurmon, from Montreal, Canada, ~~was put~~ put an advertisement in the newspaper. It said: "Ladies–write to me if you are bored with the man in your life." He received a reply from his wife.
- e Harrison Ford has several false teeth. Ford told the truth about his teeth after he was voted sexiest man alive in a popular magazine.
- f Hollywood star, Tom Duffy, has been seen with his new girlfriend, the glamorous Dolores Barker. The happy couple ~~was being visited~~ was visiting Trinidad for a short vacation.

Vocabulary

1

- a photogenic
- b obsessed
- c unflattering
- d desperate
- e insensitive
- f hypocritical

2

- a insensitive
- b desperate
- c photogenic
- d obsessed
- e hypocritical
- f unflattering

3

- a Hot Gossip
- b Parking Ticket
- c Fugitives!
- d Paparazzi Chase
- e Stop, Thief
- f Family Court

4

- a arrested
- b stolen
- c committed
- d kidnapped
- e escaped

5

- 1 great
- 2 news
- 3 Actually
- 4 thing
- 5 touch
- 6 Talking
- 7 Anyway
- 8 Guess
- 9 let
- 10 Love

6

Conversation 1

- a 2
- b 3
- c 5
- d 4
- e 1

Conversation 2

a 4
b 2
c 1
d 3

Conversation 3

a 1
b 4
c 3
d 2

Pronunciation

2

a want to think
b promise to change
c forget about it
d just doing a job
e what are you going to do about it
f was it your first time

Writing

2

a despite
b However
c Although
d Although
e despite
f However

3

a opinion
b believe
c remember
d wrong
e point
f more
g considered
h conclusion

8 Travel

Grammar

1

Country A – Venezuela
Country B – Brazil
Country C – Cuba

2

Country A

a couldn't
b might
c guess
d definitely

Country B

a certainly
b couldn't
c could
d must

3

a 6
b 5
c 2
d 4
e 1
f 7
g 3
h 8

4

a had already sold
b thought
c went
d had decided
e fell
f had invited
g met
h had never been

Vocabulary

1

a
1 in
2 of
3 far
4 in
b
5 on
6 not
c
7 to
8 on
d
9 between
10 of

b is shown in the picture.

2

a Buddhist
b snow-capped
c ancient
d waterfall
e skyline
f high-rise

3

1 surrounded
2 popular
3 lounge chairs
4 unspoiled
5 views
6 cliffs
7 southern
8 hidden
9 overlooking

4

a peace and quiet
b take it or leave it
c neat and tidy
d give or take
e all or nothing
f come and go
g sooner or later

5

a Subway station 3
b Subway station 2
c Subway station 4

Pronunciation

1

a author fall saw water
b person curving worst first
c heart garden arm market

2

/ɔ/	/ɜr/	/ɑr/
all ball bought wall water	birds girl return surf world	car hardly large part start

Listening

1

a	b	c	d	e	f
☹	☺	☹	☹	☺	☺

2

Topic	Speaker
entertainment	Speaker 2
food	Speaker 5
hotel	Speaker 3
trip	Speaker 4
money and prices	Speaker 1
weather	Speaker 6

Pronunciation

1

- a own
- b going
- c love

2

/ɔɪ/	/aʊ/	/oʊ/
enjoy	found	grow
noise	how	hole
point	our	know
toilet	proud	own
toy	round	won't

Listening

1

- a 2
- b 5
- c 6
- d 3
- e 8
- f 1
- g 7
- h 4

2

- a I didn't have a clue
- b the biggest trouble-maker
- c as if it was my fault
- d there was still no sign of her
- e there was nothing for me to do but to go and find them both myself
- f as good as gold

3 **I think that the worst experience <u>that</u> I've ever had was in my first year of teaching, and the kids knew that I didn't have a clue how to control them. I was giving the students a French test, a subject <u>that</u> most of them hated. I had a class of eighth graders and these children do anything <u>that</u> they can to give you a hard time. It's the age group <u>that</u> I find the most difficult.**

11 Age

Grammar

1

- a I wish I hadn't started smoking.
- b If only I could go on vacation.
- c If only I had told her the truth.
- d I wish I didn't have so much homework.
- e I wish I had learned to swim.
- f I wish it wasn't raining.

2

- a I wish I didn't have so many regrets.
- b I wish I had a lot of money.
- c I wish I could find time to read.
- d I wish I had paid attention in class yesterday.
- e I wish I hadn't overslept this morning.
- f I wish I hadn't eaten too much for dinner last night.
- g I wish I was good at sports.
- h I wish I didn't feel anxious all the time.

3

- a would you live
- b didn't need
- c would you change
- d would you say
- e were
- f changed
- g had
- h would they be

4

- a If I understood, I would / 'd be able to explain.
- b If I didn't feel tired, I would go out tonight.
- c If I weren't in love, I wouldn't think about him all the time.
- d If I were a liar, I wouldn't tell the truth.
- e If I could dance, I would go to nightclubs.
- f If I didn't love Coldplay, I wouldn't buy all their albums.
- g If I didn't have five children, I wouldn't spend a lot of time cooking.

5

- a would have gotten
- b had gone
- c would have gone
- d had not / hadn't worked
- e would not have worked / wouldn't have worked
- f would have been
- g would have had

Vocabulary

1

- a hopefully
- b Actually
- c Apparently
- d Predictably
- e basically
- f unbelievably
- g Fortunately

2

- 1 definitely
- 2 Personally
- 3 basically
- 4 Clearly
- 5 stupidly
- 6 Unfortunately
- 7 Apparently
- 8 Hopefully

3

- a I don't go out a lot.
- b I can't drive very well.
- c I don't enjoy going to concerts very much.
- d I don't remember my childhood very well.
- e I see my family a lot.
- f I live my life very sensibly.
- g I don't go abroad very much.
- h I like singing rock songs very loudly.

4

a Hold on, please. I'll try to put you through. ... I'm afraid he's on the other line. Would you like to hold? <u>3</u>

Oh, hi. Is Tony there, please? <u>2</u>

Hello. <u>1</u>

Yes, thank you. <u>4</u>

b Speaking. Who's calling, please? <u>3</u>

Good morning. Clyde Interiors. Can I help you? <u>1</u>

Hello. I'd like to speak to Don, please. <u>2</u>

This is Miranda, from *Perfect Home* magazine. <u>4</u>

c Tom, hold on. Can you call me back in five minutes? <u>5</u>

Joanna? Hi, it's me. <u>2</u>

Hi, Tom. Listen, I can't talk now. <u>3</u>

Hello. <u>1</u>

Just a quick question, OK? What are you doing later? <u>4</u>

d Certainly. Are you available later on today? <u>4</u>

Hello. My name is Mike Birdsell. 2

Hello. This is Eva Gomez. Can I help you? 1

Oh, yes, Mr. Birdsell. Thank you for getting back so quickly. We need to have a meeting. 3

Pronunciation

1

Speaker 2

Writing

1

1	2	3	4	5	6
a	f	d	c	e	b

12 Style

Grammar

1

- a You would look great in a little black dress.
- b I can't believe he wears his old blue jeans to work!
- c I love my Brazilian leather purse.
- d How many patterned silk scarfs do you own?
- e He always wears enormous woolen sweaters.
- f I don't think you should wear an orange top with that long purple skirt.
- g Not many people look good in shiny gold, leopard-print hot pants, but she does.

2

- a an old, snakeskin cowboy belt
- b a pair of black leather motorcycle boots
- c a pair of ridiculous, baggy silk pants
- d a large, checked baseball cap
- e an old-fashioned brown cotton shirt
- f a brand-new colorful Italian tie
- g a long, plain black leather coat

3

- a I had it sharpened.
- b She has it washed.
- c We had it painted.
- d They had it done by a builder.
- e She has it designed by a professional.
- f She has it colored at the hairdresser.
- g I had them whitened by a dentist.

4

- a have my coat mended
- b fixed the leak
- c having her wedding dress made
- d having the house cleaned
- e laid new tiles
- f have our nails done
- g have your ears tested

5

- a How often do you have your hair cut?
- b Have you ever had your ears pierced?
- c When last did you have your eyes tested?
- d Would you like to have your home redecorated?
- e Have you ever had a pair of pants taken up?
- f Where do you have your shoes repaired?
- g Have you ever had your picture taken by a professional photographer?

Vocabulary

1

Clothes	Materials	Adjective to describe clothes
belt	cotton	baggy
dress	fur	checked
jeans	leather	long-sleeved
shirt	linen	low-waisted
suit	silk	pinstriped
sweater	snakeskin	plain
sweatshirt	suede	scruffy
top	wool	stylish

2

a

1 slim
2 wavy
3 streaks
4 receding
5 deep-set
6 sideburns
7 freckles
8 mole

b

1 built
2 tattoo
3 bald
4 forehead
5 goatee
6 mustache
7 eyeliner

3

1 makes
2 turn
3 taking
4 getting
5 get
6 do
7 turn
8 having
9 making
10 doing

4

1 try
2 fits
3 look
4 wear
5 get
6 put
7 go
8 match
9 look

5

1 Thank
2 welcome
3 beautiful
4 think
5 much
6 mention
7 delicious
8 glad

Listening

1

b his career ✓

2

a T
b F
c F
d T
e T
f F
g T
h F

3

- a a story about becoming wealthy ✓
- b he has become even more successful ✓
- c that makes him special ✓
- d he had a natural talent for noticing ✓
- e Lauren has everything that anyone could want ✓

Notes

Notes

ISBN 9786685732368